D0458548

Dedicated to all those people who have chosen a career in sales.
Selling is unique. . .it is the only field where one is paid to be rejected.
To succeed, it takes a special person, but even the very best will get down occasionally. A salesperson once said:
"I am like a storage battery constantly discharging energy, and unless I am recharged at frequent intervals, I soon run dry."

That is what this book is all about. . . recharging batteries.

*This book was compiled by someone
who truly believes in the power of
words and how they can impact
feelings and attitudes.
The quotations were collected
over a period of years,
and until now only shared
with a few close friends
and associates. All of the authors
are not known; however,
we wish to acknowledge them,
whoever they may be.*

*We hope you enjoy the quotations
as much as we do.*

Copyright © 1984, Great Quotations, Inc. ISBN: 0-931089-00-X

"The quality of a person's life is in direct proportion to their commitment to excellence, regardless of their chosen field of endeavor."

Vincent T. Lombardi

"It is a funny thing about life; if you refuse to accept anything but the best, you very often get it."

Somerset Maugham

"Small opportunities are often the beginning of great enterprises."

Demosthenes

"All things are difficult before they are easy."

John Norley

"The best executive is the one
who has sense enough to
pick good men to do what
he wants done,
and self-restraint enough to
keep from meddling with
them while they do it."

"Our chief want in life is somebody who will make us do what we can."

Ralph Waldo Emerson

"The speed of the leader determines the rate of the pack."

"Adversity reveals
genius, prosperity
conceals it."

Horace

"The price of
greatness
is responsibility."

Winston Churchill

"Man's mind, once stretched by a new idea, never regains its original dimensions."

Oliver Wendell Holmes

"Destiny is not a
matter of chance,
it is a matter of
choice."

"People forget how fast
you did a job—
but they remember
how well you did it."

Howard W. Newton

"The reward of a thing well done is to have done it."

Ralph Waldo Emerson

"The future belongs to those who believe in the beauty of their dreams."

Eleanor Roosevelt

"Happiness lies in the joy of achievement and the thrill of creative effort."

Franklin Roosevelt

"There is one thing stronger than all the armies in the world, and that is an Idea whose time has come."

Victor Hugo

M16

"Accept the challenges,
so that you may feel the
exhilaration of victory."

General George S. Patton

"Do not follow where
the path may lead.

Go instead where there is
no path and leave a trail."

"Genius is one percent inspiration and ninety-nine percent perspiration."

Thomas Alva Edison

"It is one of the most beautiful compensations of this life that no man can sincerely try to help another without helping himself."

Ralph Waldo Emerson

"The highest reward for a person's toil is not what they get for it, but what they become by it."

John Ruskin

"The difference between ordinary and extraordinary is that little extra."

'Luck is what happens when preparation meets opportunity.''

Elmer Letterman

"No problem can stand the assault of sustained thinking."

Voltaire

"There is something that is much more scarce, something rarer than ability.

It is the ability to recognize ability."

Robert Half

"Progress always involves risk; you can't steal second base and keep your foot on first."

Frederick Wilcox

"Success is simply a matter of luck.

Ask any failure."

Earl

Did is a word of achievement,
Won't is a word of retreat,
Might is a word of bereavement,
Can't is a word of defeat,
Ought is a word of duty,
Try is a word each hour,
Will is a word of beauty,
Can is a word of power.

"Do not wish to be anything
 but what you are,
 and try to be
 that perfectly."

St. Francis De Sales

"I do the best I know how,
the very best I can; and I mean to
keep on doing it to the end.

If the end brings me out all right,
what is said against me will not
amount to anything.

If the end brings me out all wrong,
ten angels swearing I was right
would make no difference."

Abraham Lincoln

"One hour of life, crowded to the full with glorious action, and filled with noble risks, is worth whole years of those mean observances of paltry decorum, in which men steal through existence, like sluggish waters through a marsh, without either honour or observation."

Sir Walter Scott

M31

"If a man is called to be a
streetsweeper, he should sweep streets
even as Michelangelo painted,
or Beethoven composed music,
or Shakespeare wrote poetry.
   He should sweep streets so well
that all the hosts of heaven and earth
will pause to say, here lived a great
streetsweeper who did his job well."

Martin Luther King, Jr.

"The worst bankrupt in
the world is the person who
has lost his enthusiasm."

H.W. Arnold

"Many receive advice,
only the wise profit
from it."

Syrus

Winner vs. Loser

The Winner—is always part of the answer;
The Loser—is always part of the problem;
The Winner—always has a program;
The Loser—always has an excuse;
The Winner—says "Let me do it for you;"
The Loser—says "That's not my job;"
The Winner—sees an answer for
              every problem;
The Loser—sees a problem for every answer;
The Winner—sees a green near every
              sand trap;
The Loser—sees two or three sand traps
              near every green;
The Winner—says, "It may be difficult but
              it's possible;"
The Loser—says, "It may be possible but
              it's too difficult."

Be A Winner

"Chance favors the prepared mind."

Louis Pasteur

"When we have done
our best, we should
wait the result
in peace."

J. Lubbock

"When two men in
a business always agree,
one of them
is unnecessary."

Make no little plans;
They have no magic to stir
  men's blood
And probably themselves will not
  be realized.
Make big plans; aim high
  in hope and work,
Remembering that a noble,
  logical diagram
Once recorded will not die.

Daniel H. Burnham

"A single conversation across
the table with a wise man
is worth a month's study
of books."

Chinese Proverb

"The only good luck many great men ever had was being born with the ability and determination to overcome bad luck."

Channing Pollock

"Far away there in the sunshine
are my highest aspirations.
I may not reach them, but I can
look up and see their beauty,
believe in them and try to
follow where they lead."

Louisa May Alcott

"You will become as small as your controlling desire; as great as your dominant aspiration."

James Allen

"When you hire people who are smarter than you are, you prove you are smarter than they are."

R.H. Grant

"Live your life each day as you
would climb a mountain.

An occasional glance toward the
summit keeps the goal in mind,
but many beautiful scenes are
to be observed from each new
vantage point.

Climb slowly, steadily, enjoying
each passing moment; and the view
from the summit will serve as a
fitting climax for the journey."

Harold V. Melchert

"Obstacles are those frightful things you see when you take your eyes off your goals."

"Genius is the ability to reduce the complicated to the simple."

C.W. Ceran

"Things may come to those who wait, but only the things left by those who hustle."

Abraham Lincoln

"To love what you do and feel that it matters—how could anything be more fun?"

Katharine Graham

"Winners expect to win in advance.

Life is a self-fulfilling prophecy."

"Don't wait for your ship to come in, swim out to it."

"There's no thrill in easy sailing
when the skies are clear and blue,
there's no joy in merely doing things
which any one can do.

But there is some satisfaction
that is mighty sweet to take,
when you reach a destination that
you thought you'd never make."

Spirella

"A great pleasure in life
is doing what people say
you cannot do."

Walter Gagehot

"The man who believes
he can do something
is probably right, and
so is the man who believes
he can't."

"One man with courage makes a majority."

Andrew Jackson

"We are continually faced
by great opportunities
brilliantly disguised as
insoluble problems."

"When nothing seems to help,
I go and look at a stonecutter
hammering away at his rock perhaps
a hundred times without as much as
a crack showing in it.

Yet at the hundred and first blow
it will split in two, and I know it
was not that blow that did it—
but all that had gone before."

Jacob Riis

"The difference between
a successful person and others
is not a lack of strength,
not a lack of knowledge,
but rather in a lack of will."

Vincent T. Lombardi

"Yesterday is a cancelled
check;
tomorrow is a promissory
note;
today is the only cash
you have—
so spend it wisely."

Kay Lyons

"In great attempts
it is glorious even
to fail."

"Quality is never an accident;
it is always the result of high
intention, sincere effort, intelligent
direction and skillful execution;
it represents the wise choice of
many alternatives."

Willa A. Foster

"As I grow older,
 I pay less attention
 to what men say.

I just watch what
they do."

Andrew Carnegie

"The credit belongs to the man who
is actually in the arena, whose face is
marred by dust and sweat and blood;
who strives valiantly; who errs and comes
short again and again, who knows the
great enthusiasms, the great devotions,
and spends himself in a worthy cause;
who at the best, knows the triumph
of high achievement; and who,
at the worst, if he fails, at least
fails while daring greatly, so that his
place shall never be with those cold and
timid souls who know neither victory
nor defeat."

Theodore Roosevelt

M63

''Nothing in the world can take the place of persistence.

Talent will not; nothing is more common than unsuccessful men with talent. Genius will not; unrewarded genius is almost a proverb.

Education will not; the world is full of educated derelicts.

Persistence and determination alone are omnipotent.

Calvin Coolidge

"The people who get on in
this world are the people
who get up and look for the
circumstances they want,
and, if they can't find them,
make them."

George Bernard Shaw

"Failures are divided into
two classes—
    those who thought and
never did,
    and those who did and
never thought."

John Charles Salak

"The man who wins may
have been counted out
several times,
but he didn't hear
the referee."

H.E. Jansen

"The secret of happiness
is not in doing what one
likes, but in liking what
one does."

James M. Barrie

"He who believes is strong;
he who doubts is weak.

Strong convictions precede
great actions."

J.F. Clarke

"Winning is not a sometime thing;
it's an all time thing.

You don't win once in a while,
you don't do things right
once in a while, you do them
right all the time.

Winning is a habit.

Unfortunately, so is losing."

Vince Lombardi

"Failure is the opportunity to begin again more intelligently."

Henry Ford

"Well done
is better than
well said."

Ben Franklin

"Success is a journey,
not a destination."

Ben Sweetland

Order Your Favorite Quote Today!

Timeless... Your favorite quote on a beautiful brass plate mounted on a walnut finished base. A real conversation piece for your home or office.

"The quality of a
Person's life is
In direct proportion
To their commitment
To excellence,
Regardless of their
Chosen field of
Endeavor."

PRICE LIST

	BRASS PLAQUE
	Beautiful brass plate mounted on walnut finished base. Outside dimensions - 8 x 10.
1	**$25.00**
2-10	**$19.00**
11-25	**$17.00**

Over 25: please call for custom quote.

Shipping and handling:
Add $3.00 per unit on quantities of 1-10.
Add $2.50 per unit on quantities of 11-25.

MAIL ORDER FORM TO:

GREAT QUOTATIONS, INC.
919 SPRINGER DRIVE • LOMBARD, IL 60148-6416

TOLL FREE: 800-621-1432
(708) 953-1222

ORDER FORM

QTY	PRODUCT	QUOTE PAGE NUMBER	UNIT PRICE	TOTAL PRICE

MAIL ORDER FORM TO:

SUBTOTAL	$	
6 ¼ % SALES TAX (IL RES.)	$	
SHIPPING & HANDLING	$	
TOTAL	$	

GREAT QUOTATIONS, INC.
919 Springer Drive
Lombard, Illinois 60148-6416
Local (708) 953-1222
Toll-Free 800-621-1432

NAME _____

ADDRESS _____

CITY_____ STATE_____ ZIP_____

Phone Number ( ) _____
Enclosed is my check or money order for $ made
out to Great Quotations, Inc.
Charge my ☐ VISA   ☐ MASTER CARD
Card Number_____Exp. date_____
Signature _____

Other Great Quotations Books:

- Happy Birthday
- Best of Success
- Great Quotes/
  Great Leaders
- Aged to Perfection
- Retirement
- Love on Your
  Wedding…
- Thank You
- Thinking of You
- Words of Love
- Words for Friendship
- To My Love
- Inspirations
- Sports Quotes

- Never Never Quit
- Motivational Quotes
- Customer Care
- Commitment to
  Quality
- Over the Hill
- Golf Humor
- Happy Birthday
  to the Golfer
- Handle Stress
- Great Quotes/
  Great Women
- Humorous Quotes
- Keys to Happiness
- Things You'll Learn…

GREAT QUOTATIONS, INC.
919 SPRINGER DRIVE • LOMBARD, IL 60148-6416

TOLL FREE: 800-621-1432
(708) 953-1222